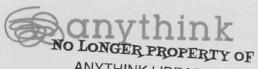

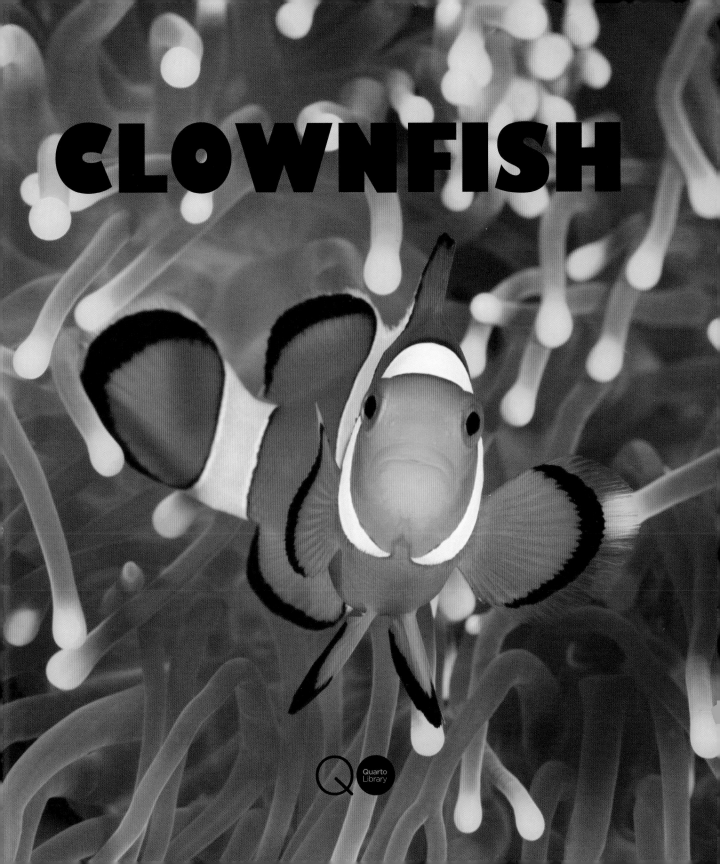

CLOWNFISH

Quarto
Library

Quarto is the authority on a wide range of topics.

Quarto educates, entertains and enriches the lives of
our readers—enthusiasts and lovers of hands-on living.

www.quartoknows.com

Design: Duck Egg Blue
Editor: Joanna McInerney

This library edition published in 2017 by Quarto Library.,
Part of The Quarto Group
6 Orchard, Lake Forest, CA 92630

© 2017 QEB Publishing, Published by Quarto Library.,
an imprint of Quarto Publishing Group USA Inc.

Distributed in the United States and Canada by
Lerner Publisher Services
241 First Avenue North
Minneapolis, MN 55401 U.S.A.
www.lernerbooks.com

A CIP record for this book is available from the Library of Congress.

ISBN 978 1 68297 082 9

Printed in China

Contents

What is a clownfish?

Clownfish are small, colorful fish that live in **coral reefs**. They are unusual fish because they can live inside a sea anemone—an animal that stings fish and eats them. Sea anemones don't sting clownfish. Instead, these ocean animals live together, with an amazing type of friendship.

Living underwater

Clownfish live in the sea and use **gills** to breathe underwater. Their bodies are a good shape for swimming, and **fins** help them to move around and change direction.

That's amazing!

The most famous clownfish are called clown anemonefish. They are bright orange, with three wide white bands that are trimmed in black. They can grow to about 4 inches (10 cm) long.

Types of clownfish

Most clownfish are orange, red, brown, black, or yellow. They have bands of white, but some types have different colors, or patches of color instead. Most clownfish are less than 6 inches (15 cm) long. Female clownfish are usually bigger than males.

Different colors

Barrier reef anemonefish are black with blue bands. Tomato clownfish are orange or red with just one band of white, near their heads. Skunk clownfish are yellow, with no bands of color.

That's amazing!

There are about 30 different types of clownfish. A group of clownfish is called a school, and they sometimes live as families in one sea anemone.

One little home

Most clownfish live with one sea anemone in a coral reef. They can find all the food they need there, and the sea anemone keeps them safe from other animals.

Coral reefs

Clownfish live in coral reefs. These are rocky places under the sea that are made by tiny animals called coral polyps. Coral polyps only live in warm, salty, clean water. Reefs are found in shallow water, near to land. They are full of colorful animals and plants.

That's amazing!

When a clownfish finds a sea anemone it wants to live in, it does a special dance called a wiggle dance. As it dances, the fish moves the water around the anemone, helping it to breathe!

Sea anemones

A sea anemone looks like a flower, but it is a small, soft animal that sticks itself to a coral reef. It has a single hole at the top of its tubelike body. It uses this hole both to eat and to expel waste. There are rows of soft, bendy **tentacles** around the anemone's mouth.

Stinging tentacles

The tentacles on a sea anemone have little stingers that can fire deadly **venom** into a fish. When a fish passes by, it gets caught and stung by the tentacles.

That's amazing!

An anemone's sting starts to work quickly. It stops a fish from being able to move, so it cannot escape. The anemone uses its tentacles to push the fish into its mouth.

That's amazing!

Sea anemones, coral polyps, and **jellyfish** belong to the same family of ocean animals. They all have stinging tentacles that they use to catch their **prey.**

Staying safe

A clownfish can stay safe inside a sea anemone because the anemone doesn't sting it. The fish has a thick layer of **mucus** covering its body and this makes it **invisible** to the anemone. Even if the anemone does sting a clownfish, the mucus protects it from harm.

Hiding from danger

If a bigger fish sees a clownfish and begins to chase it, the clownfish dives deep into its anemone's tentacles. It is safe from attack because the **predator** will be stung if it comes too close.

What clownfish eat

Clownfish find food floating around a sea anemone's tentacles, and eat it. The food is leftovers from the anemone's last meal! This keeps the sea anemone healthy and clean, because otherwise bits of old food could get trapped around its body.

Types of food

Clownfish also eat small animals in the ocean. They can catch and eat creatures similar to **shrimp** that swim past them. Some clownfish also eat tiny sea plants, called **algae**.

That's amazing!

If there is no food floating around the anemone, a clownfish won't go hungry. It can nibble on the anemone's tentacles instead —and the anemone still won't sting it!

Baby fish

A female clownfish lays her eggs close to her sea anemone. She lays them on a **nest**, which is a rocky place that she and her mate have cleaned first. A group of eggs is called a clutch. A clownfish can lay more than 1,000 eggs in a clutch.

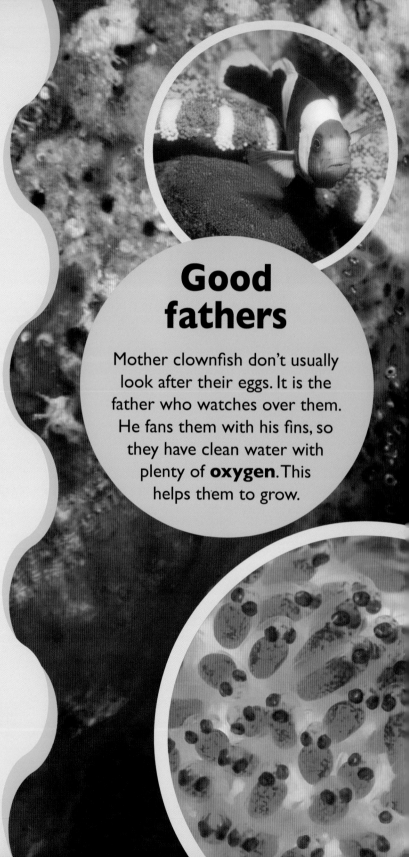

Good fathers

Mother clownfish don't usually look after their eggs. It is the father who watches over them. He fans them with his fins, so they have clean water with plenty of **oxygen**. This helps them to grow.

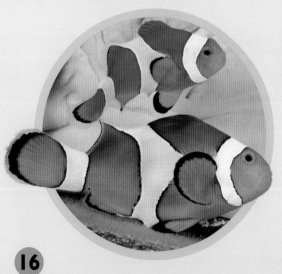

That's amazing!

The eggs are ready to **hatch** in just one to two weeks. The baby fish are called fry, and when they hatch they are all males! Some of them will turn into females as they get older.

Family life

Clownfish live together as a family. The leader is a female, who lays all the eggs. There is only one male that can mate with her, but there are other, younger males who live with them too. When baby fish hatch, they are swept away by the **water currents** and make new homes.

That's amazing!

If a mother clownfish dies, one of the male fish will turn into a female, and he takes her place as the leader of the family!

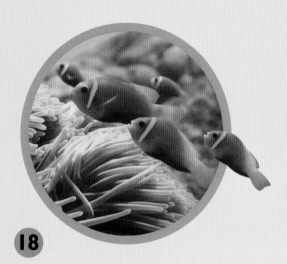

Keep out!

Clownfish do not like to share
their anemone with other fish,
apart from their own family.
If another fish comes too close,
they make loud sounds to scare
it away. If that doesn't work,
a clownfish will attack
the **invader**.

Aquariums

An aquarium is a large tank filled with water. People who collect fish keep them in aquariums, so they can enjoy watching them. Most of the clownfish that people keep as pets have been taken from coral reefs.

That's amazing!

The Great Barrier Reef on the Australian coast is the world's largest coral reef. It can be seen from space! Millions of people visit it every year to see clownfish and other sea life.

People and clownfish

Clownfish live in coral reefs, and humans are damaging these precious places. People turn the seawater dirty by putting bad things in it, such as oil or trash. When the water is dirty, we say it is **polluted**. Coral polyps quickly die in polluted water.

21

Glossary

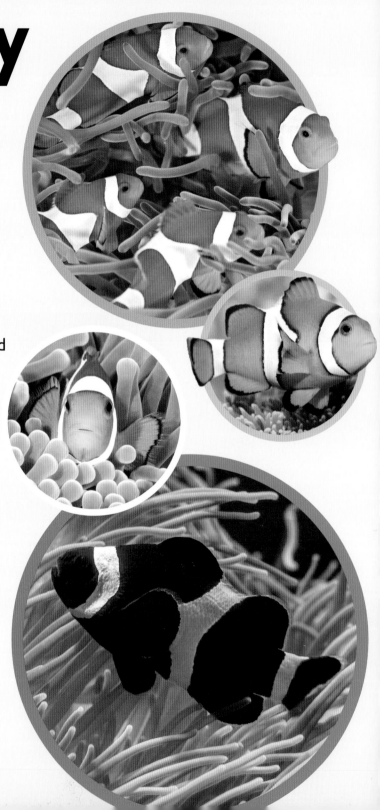

Algae

Algae are plants that live in the sea. Seaweeds are algae.

Coral reef

This is a rocky area in the sea made by little animals called polyps.

Fins

Fish have fins on their bodies instead of arms or legs. They use them to swim.

Gills

Fish have gills to breathe instead of lungs.

Hatch

This is when an egg breaks open, so the baby animal can get out.

Invader

An invader is an animal that comes into another animal's space.

Invisible

Something that is invisible cannot be seen.

Jellyfish

This is a soft-bodied animal with a bell-like body and long tentacles.

Mucus

Mucus is a jelly-like thick layer that is made by the fish's skin.

Nest

A nest is where animals put their eggs to keep them safe.

Oxygen

Oxygen is in air and water. Animals breathe so they can get oxygen into their bodies.

Polluted

When water becomes dirty it is polluted.

Predator

A predator is an animal that hunts other animals.

Prey

Animals that are hunted are called prey.

Shrimp

A shrimp is a small ocean animal with ten legs.

Tentacles

Tentacles are long, thin, and soft. An animal can move its tentacles.

Venom

Venom is a poison that an animal makes to defend itself, or to hurt or kill prey.

Water currents

Water flows under the oceans, just like it flows in rivers. This is called a current.

Index

Picture credits

(t=top, b=bottom, l=left, r=right, fc=front cover, bc=back cover)

Alamy

1 Zoonar GmbH, 4r Wolfgang Pölzer, 6b, 10-11, 16t Jane Gould, 6t Jeffrey Warrington, 6-7, 14-15l imageBROKER, 7bl Iakov Filimonov, 8-9 Joe Belanger, 12-13 Ethan Daniels, 13cl ellejay, 14b Luca Frontini, 16b Poelzer Wolfgang, 16-17 RGB Ventures / SuperStock, 18-19, 19tl Reinhard Dirscherl,

Seapics

4-5 James D. Watt

Shutterstock

2 Sphinx Wang, 2-3 Andrey_Kuzmin, 4bl and 22l cbpix, 5 and 22r, 15bl Kletr, 8l Isantilli, 9l and 22b Victor Wong, 9b Volodymyr Goinyk, 10b 13b volkan yenel, 10b, 14-15 Andrea Izzotti, 11r Frank Wasserfuehrer, 12b buttchi 3 Sha Life, 14-15, 16b SARAWUT KUNDEJ, 18bl Sergey Novikov, 18br and 22t Krzysztof Odziomek, 20b Jordan Tan, 20-21 Levent Konuk, 21b Ethan Daniels